God bless you and keep you, brother. May you be surrounded in the truth of who God is, and may the smallest of His truths remain profound to you. May the voice of child-like faith never leave you.

through Christ, all things,

Spiritually Speaking

Vol. I

Alex Anderson
2019

Copyright © 2019 by Alex Anderson

All rights reserved. This book or any portion thereof may not be reproduced or used in any manner whatsoever without the express written permission of the publisher except for the use of brief quotations in a book review.

Printed in the United States of America
First printing: 2019
ISBN 978-0-359-81663-7

Table of Contents

Great Lights	1
I Believe	2
Praise God	3
God Will Help Us	4
Multi-Colored Signs of God	5
Your Lighthouse	6
Untitled (Resurrection)	7
Jesus's Promise	8
The Lord's Table	9
Faith Alone	10
When I Deny The Glorious Lord	11
The Peace of Galilee	12
God Knows	17
The Ears of Night	18
Come to Jesus	19
The Last Charge (Mark 5:25-34)	20
He is Here	21
Man of Sorrows	22
Christmas Birth	23
God's Majesty and Me	24

God over the Waters	25
A Good Friday	26
The Lowly Son of God	27
Easter's Substance	28
Thief On The Left	29
The Kid on Christmas	30
God Lets Himself In	31
Greater Love	32
Like Christ	33
Just	34
In Reflection	35

Introduction

This year marks two decades since I started writing poetry, which is crazy for me to think about. Looking back at 20 years of work, there are poems I would consider more notable than others, depending on their context, topic, or construction. Our lists of which poems are noteworthy probably differ but regardless, I have been blessed with an ability to explore many intellectual and emotional worlds through writing and have been humbled by the people who have joined me on that ride.

All journeys have beginnings, and mine starts as a young boy who gave his life to Jesus Christ. When I was exposed to Shel Silverstein's writing a little bit later, poetry came naturally through writing about my faith. These early poems have a simple quality to them, a straightforward innocence, which has been difficult to replicate over the years. (That young boy has never left, but he often now competes with his older self's ideas, experiences, and habits.)

The truth is, sometimes it's hard to believe things simply, like a child. Adulthood teaches us how to live complex lives, and when beliefs or behaviors lack that complexity, it can be seen as immature. Because of that, you may find certain poems in this book "childish" in the way society negatively defines that word. Whether it is by design or circumstance, however, I have found it easier to find God and grasp His nature by simple thinking. And the best way to capture simple thoughts is through simple writing.

My identity may appear different through my statements, my writing, or my actions, so where I fail to express it strong enough elsewhere, let it be known here— underneath it all, this is who I am. I am nothing without Christ, who for some reason extends grace to me in spite of my insistence that my ways are better than His. It's God who deserves any glory from my writing, which is another reason why I've chosen to acknowledge my decades of work through poetry about Him.

I am excited to show this side— this child— of me to you. And I hope you too, child of God, follow after Him.

"...but these are written so that you may believe that Jesus is the Christ, the Son of God, and that by believing you may have life in his name."

John 20:31 (ESV)

Great Lights

I looked up at the moon,
he looked down at me
He shone on the grass,
the trees,
and the sea
God is so loving,
He sends us a great light—
In the morning it's the sun,
And the moon at night
He added the stars also,
to finish off His beauty
To stop and look at His wonders
and thank Him is our duty.

1.14.02

I Believe

I believe Jesus died,
I believe He was crucified.
I believe that He rose again
to beat death and save Man from sin.
I believe it was God's plan,
'cause sin separated God from Man.
So, God sent His only son
Jesus, the Perfect One.

Why did Jesus come to our globe?
So people would believe (when the message goes through their earlobe).
When you ask Him into your heart and say "amen",
You will live forever in Heaven!
I don't just believe that, I know
'Cause it says in the Bible, and I believe it so!

8.10.02 (re-worked 2019)

Praise God

The sun is out, so I go out to play
I think to myself, "What a beautiful day!"
God made this day a good one—
"Thank you God, and your Son!"

The next day, the rain is out
I sit in my chair, ready to pout
Then I think about yesterday—
"I should praise God anyway!"
"Thank you God, for another day,
even if I can't go out to play
I will play inside for today—
and I hope tomorrow will be a nicer day!"

8.21.02

God Will Help Us

Though Satan should tempt us in every way,
God will help us every day
God gave us the Bible, which is God's word,
and that word Satan does not want heard
So even when Satan tempts us every day,
We have the Bible, and we can also pray!

9.10.02

Multi-Colored Signs of God

The rain came down hard, then it ended slow
I looked up in the sky, and saw a rainbow
Different kinds of colors fill the sky above
I know the one who made it is a God of peace and love
He is the Alpha, Omega, Jehovah, Great I Am,
He is the Messiah, Savior, the Perfect Lamb
He is the Beginning and End, Jesus, God's Son,
And we should praise Him every day
for He has made us every one!

10.01.02

Your Lighthouse

When the sun comes up and lights the land,
You can see a lighthouse, magnificent it stands
It shines for lost ships during the night
It also turns darkness into light
Jesus is our lighthouse in the night
If He lives in you, you will shine so bright
You can take out the darkness and it will go away
And with God's help, you will not be led astray
Jesus is a lighthouse for me and for you
Like a lighthouse, He helps lost people too

10.16.02

Untitled (Resurrection)

In a grave His body lay
He rose from death on the 3rd day
And now He sits at the right hand
of the God who rules the land

Christ conquered sin and of course the grave
because He came to the Earth to save
Now Jesus Christ has victory
and Satan is lost for eternity
My eyes are open, I clearly see
that Christ has died for you and me

While we're on Earth He watches above
to see who will accept His love

3.18.04

Jesus's Promise

Give me your weak and heavy laden
Give me your men stricken with grief
Give me a hurt and broken maiden
Give me a righteous man labeled "a thief"

Give me a Believer who is fighting terror
Give me a Godly man who is beaten and bruised
Give me a struggler who is overcoming his error
Give me a persistent one who has walked in Christ's shoes

Give me a Christian who feels undone
One who feels his torments will never cease
Give him to me, God's one and only Son
Give them all to me, and I shall give them peace

8.18.05

The Lord's Table

Thank you for this bread
That symbolizes your body broken
Lord, you came to forgive what I've said
And what I've said without it being spoken
Your body was inflicted with great pain
You were cut, crippled, and bruised
You saved us while we had nothing to gain
We had nothing to gain; we had everything to lose

Thank you for this wine
It symbolizes your blood shed
Lord, you gave your life to save mine
You did not resist while you suffered and bled
To us your blood was poured
Water and soap cannot wash us clean
We are not saved by our own accord
Our ways are twisted, our mouths obscene

Lord, your table is a remembrance
Of what we can never hope to accomplish
We all are dead; we all need deliverance
We've been born grimy; a cracked and dirty dish
I'm a boy, and I am not faultless
What I hope to be is not what I've been
My decision-making has left me salt-less
My Spirit is grieved with returning sin
Lord, your table has taught me anew
Of what I've heard all my days
Living isn't easy and our days are few
Praise our merciful God, who shines light into our grays

7.9.06

Faith Alone

Out of darkness and into the light
Steps hardly falter, my eyes straight ahead
I walk by faith and not by sight
And not by thoughts inside my head

Our thoughts conflict and bring to light
A dozen things we shouldn't think
They're mainly wrong and seldom right
Floating on top to make us sink

You can fight an idea, you can partly ignore
To move a step away from doubt
But those flung thoughts knock on your door
And wishes and locks won't keep them out

Things above we have to believe
Apart from ourselves, apart from our speech
Trusting what you know as you pack up and leave
Will lead you away from radiant reach

You can't see the rocks that push us aside
You can't feel the rebellion in your bone
But when your faults and fear collide,
You can only walk by faith alone

3.7.07

When I Deny The Glorious Lord

When I deny the glorious Lord
My grin is stretched out thin and wide
And as He stands with outstretched hands
I bruise and break His blameless sides

When I deny the glorious Lord
Both eager hands grasp tight the whip
Still He resigns with bending spine
While I reduce His flesh to strips

When I deny the glorious Lord
My heart's as cold as rusted nails
And as He lies with pleading eyes
I smash His wrists to wooden rails

When I deny the glorious Lord
I strike Him with my spit and scorn
And though He's slain unjust and shamed
He'd die for me a million more

3.21.08

The Peace of Galilee

Part I: The Conviction

I found a peace to set me free
along the shore of Galilee
On the water, calm He stands
with holes marked in His hands

There He stands to light the dim
amidst the strong, prevailing wind
There to pacify the pain
beneath the pelting rain

There with hope He stands to pave
even against the highest wave
To be the peace for setting free
the soul who will believe.

Part II: The Calamity

I grab my boat and start to row,
The wind is strong, the pace is slow,
Rocks jut out in scattered stance--
The waves pound hard below

What is this thing that stands ahead,
with invitation never said,
and yet His earnest, searching stare
draws me to come instead?

I wonder what He seeks to prove
Looking on, as if to soothe
While I still fight a savage storm,
And I can hardly move

The clouds turn dark and start to pour,
Water floods the wooden floor,
My intentions were to sail, not sink—
I'm heading back to shore.

Part III: The Chasm

Rowing back was not too tough,
The winds died to a silent puff
The skies turned clear
As I drew near
The waves were not that rough

Then suddenly, when all seemed sure,
The frozen figure spoke and stirred,
"Have faith in me,
And I can free
you from the things you were."

And in those words, I knew it fact
that that man held the parts I lacked
and armed with hope
I turned the boat
And started to row back

But with all strength, it was no use
As oars and boards broke from abuse
Of fresh-whipped waves
And lightning's blaze
Which loomed to tear me loose

Part IV: The Compassion

The wind resurged and hit me strong,
And with the waves that joined the throng,
I slipped and swayed and fell headlong
into the frigid sea

Darkness shook my desperate eyes,
The deep restrained my frantic cries,
while silence spoke of my demise
that I knew soon would be

And it was then, when doomed to drown,
As coldness swarmed me all around,
A pierced but mighty hand swept down
and pulled me from the grave

The man, now soaked and dripping wet,
smiled at me, as though we've met,
and I've learned since not to forget
His loving will to save

Part V: The Conclusion

I found a peace to set me free
along the shore of Galilee
On the water, calm He stands
with holes marked in His hands

Still there he stands, a steady form
against the force of any storm
With waiting hands to grab and grasp
The hopeless falling fast

Ever there, He grants the way
For living new life every day
Lifelong thanks and worship be
to Christ of Galilee!

3.30.10

God Knows

I may not be in a history book.
I may not get a second look.
I may not journey far in this land—
   But God knows who I am.

I may not have the skills of a speaker.
I may not possess the sharpest mind either.
I may not be easy to understand—
   But God knows who I am.

I may not be flawless in terms of perfection.
I may not be whole with all my affection.
At times the valley seems too grand—
   But God knows who I am.

I may not always know how to act.
I may not lead the group or pack.
I may not see where I fit in His plan—
   But God knows who I am.

(And I trust His mighty hand.)

10.6.10 (re-worked 2019)

The Ears of Night

The pillow holds my thoughts at night
The ceiling sees my prayers
My wishes prod the starry lights
And relay my hopes and cares
In sleep, all my deep dreams and visions
Console prevailing fears
I praise God Creation listens,
But thank God it's He who hears.

2.16.11

Come to Jesus

"Come to me, whose days are dreary
Come to me, whose sight is dim
Come to me, the worn and weary
Come to me, those stained by sin

Come to me, the powers humbled
Come to me, the poor and petty
Come to me, whose stride has stumbled
Come to me, whose hearts are heavy

Come to me, the child crying
Come to me, the man condemned
Come to me, the elder dying
Come to me, women and men

Come to me with what you carry
Come, and bring all your distress
Come thou troubled, and I will bear thee."

Come to Jesus, and rest.

4.24.11

The Last Charge
(Mark 5:25-34)

You may have lived with pain for years,
Your nights spent kneeled with pleading
You may have hurts for all your tears,
   And scars from all your bleeding.

You may have searched the dusty roads
   To find some solid ground
You may have tried to drop your loads
   Without help to be found.

Defeat is on your dinner plate
   Despair is at your door
You may believe God closed His gate,
   Or can't hear anymore.

Yet while you've searched for cures with coin
   Some healing can't be bought
But aid will always come to join
   the weak, when it is sought.

When hopelessness has worn you thin,
   And worsens your condition,
When crowds of doubt are closing in,
   And cloud your desperate vision,

Pursue the light, seek out His face,
   God's healing sacrifice
Reach out in faith to saving grace,
   Hold on to Jesus Christ.

9.14.11

He is Here

In the dim of despair, He was there
As the tide rushed away, He stayed
In the pit of my pain, He remained
As I trudged through the muck, He stuck.

On my sidewalks of sorrow, He followed
When running from grace, He chased
On roads the path faded, He waited
When I fled in my shame, He came

When faith turned to fear, He was near
As I started to slide, He arrived
When trust would desert me, He searched me
As my sure footing fell, He held

While peace falls to pieces, He reaches
As joy disappears, He is here
In the holes of my hopes, He is close:
I am never left alone
when I need God the most.

1.23.12

Man of Sorrows

Man of sorrows,
Who can loose the thorns upon your head?
Who can cleanse your jagged stripes
from where your body bled?
Who can shield your nakedness
and clothe your weakened flesh?
Who can ease your failing strength
from where you cannot rest?

Man of sorrows,
Who can pull the nails out from your hands?
Who can lower down your arms
from where the crossbeam spans?
Who can reinforce your legs
that struggle on the wood?
Who can offer you a drink
from where the soldiers stood?

Man of sorrows,
Who can tear your body from the cross?
Who can free your splintered-skin
from what your love has cost?
Who can silence all the men
who spit at you and sneer?
Who can re-place all your friends
who long have disappeared?

Man of sorrows,
Who can wipe the tears out of your eyes?
Who can blot out all the blood
that pours from every side?
For my dues, you suffered through
the agonies of Hell
For my sin, I enter in
and grieve with thee as well.

10.26.12

Christmas Birth

He was born inside a stable
because I was not able
to live a righteous man

He was born beside the cattle
because my soul was shackled
to the death my sins demand

He was born into a manger
because I was a stranger
and an enemy of God

He was born in tattered garments
because my heart was tarnished
and my many works were flawed

He was born inside a village
because my fallen image
was not worth thinking of

He was born upon this planet
for nothing we could merit
but because of His great love.

12.24.12

God's Majesty and Me

He lays the ground and plants the trees
   And yet, He still has care for me

He splits the sky and pours the seas
   And yet, He still has care for me

He carves the mountains, blows the breeze
He tells the streams to flow or freeze
   My God directs life's majesties–
   And yet, He cares the most for me.

5.28.13

God over the Waters

My sails are only tied by strands
My mast is just a wooden post
And I have come to distant lands
and drifted to each countless coast
But all I find are shallow shores
that only force my will aground
I scrape up hard on ocean floors
each rigid rock and sandy mound

But You concern with broken vessels
And You have care for sinking boats
If You can walk on waves I wrestle,
Then You can keep my ship afloat
And I can sail the weather yonder
And I can brave the surf that swarms
If You made light from darkest waters
And if You calm the ocean storms

So be the wind behind my sails
And be the boards beneath my craft
I fear no belly of the whales
Nor sea to swallow up my raft
Steer me to the narrow river
Lead me through the ocean reef
Direct my drifting, and deliver
Be my anchor in the deep.

12.14.13

A Good Friday

It's a good Friday,
And maybe it's the best
To have life's failing grade remade
as if I aced the test
For God's own Son took my own sins
so that I could be blessed
And all you need to do is trust Him–
He's done all the rest.

4.18.14

The Lowly Son of God

He came without a scepter,
a golden crown, or throne
Not as Divine Protector,
nor king to rule his own
He lived a humble servant,
No glory to be left
And though he did not earn it,
He died a villain's death

A child whose birth was downcast,
his bed in cattle's feed
His brother was the outcast
and those who were in need
To be the least he wallowed,
The narrow road he trod
O what a man to follow,
the lowly Son of God.

12.25.14

Easter's Substance

Love.

It isn't in you.
It isn't of you.
It is upon you.

Will you choose it?

3.27.16

Thief On The Left

I've never known
a love like that
hanging, breathless, by its bonds
draped like some outstretched umbrella
intent to challenge men and gods

I've never witnessed
blood like that
inexpensive, free as breath
so awkward in my crooked hands
I was the thief on the left

3.16.17

The Kid on Christmas

Born in a manger
Killed on a cross
Sunday's glory
Friday's loss
Lived so all souls
may be reborn–
This kid on Christmas
is Christ the Lord!

12.24.17

God Lets Himself In

People often daydream
"Well when I get to Heaven..."
as if it's basic science
what goes down must come up.
I've always heard it said though
that Heaven is where God lives
which means He lets Himself in
when He comes home from work

But I don't know the address
to His place out in the universe
How would one begin to find
the front door to His home?
It's doubtful guards would simply let
just anyone come over
I guess the important question is
How much of you is Him?

8.2.18

Greater Love

Jesus wept inside the Garden
alone, abandoned, and afraid
then served the sentence for my pardon,
walking still the way of pain.

Fully God, yet fully human
Fully conscious of these hells
What makes a man worth his own ruin?
Greater love for someone else.

9.5.18

Like Christ

To be like Christ, to be like Christ,
Oh what must I sacrifice
My scheduled days, my selfish nights
My fallen ways I once thought nice

To be like Christ, to be like Christ,
How much of me will suffice
My deepest wounds, my strongest mights
My closest friends and human rights

To be like Christ, to be like Christ,
Seems at this height too great a price
To bear a cross, a cruel device
To die each day, to be born twice
But all the wealth our planet cites
Leads to a lesser paradise
One love surpasses all delights
To be made whole:
To be like Christ

9.26.18

Just

He was just a man—
Someone from some other land
Lived like many had before
Nothing more.

It was just a cross—
A fine attempt, but awful loss
A sinner gives, a sinner gets
Nothing less.

And yet…

Suppose that just is not the case
Suppose that justice in our place
was met by just this man and cross—
God's son's paradox

And maybe Jesus wasn't just
a man who died because he must
For **my** sins pierced, for **my** sins crushed,
He was just
for us.

4.19.19

In Reflection

When I reflect upon the day
the times I may have lost my way,
I'm humbled by the sober notion:
I can't save myself

And I try to do so, in my might
I wake up early, and work all night
But even with my best devotion,
I know I need help

I'm always one step from my ruin
So each new breath I breathe, it's proven
Someone cares enough for me
to keep this soul alive

And I must put my faith in Him
to fill my God-sized flaws within
for I can never be set free
on simply how I strive.

7.4.19

Lord, be my life!

This is where your story continues...